That Isn't You

That Isn't You

John B. Lee

Hidden Brook Press
www.HiddenBrookPress.com
EST. 1994

A Legacy Book Publishing company

Copyright © 2022 John B. Lee
Copyright © 2022 Hidden Brook Press

All rights revert to the author. All rights for book, layout and design remain with the publisher. No part of this book may be reproduced except by a reviewer who may quote brief passages in a review. The use of any part of this publication reproduced, transmitted in any form or by any means, electronic, mechanical, photocopied, recorded or otherwise stored in a retrieval system without prior permission in writing from the author or publisher.

Title: That Isn't You
Author: John B. Lee
Editor: John B. Lee
Publisher: Hidden Brook Press - a Legacy Book Publishing company
Cover Design: Legacy Book Publishing
Layout and Design: Legacy Book Publishing

Typeset in Garamond
Printed and bound in Canada

Library and Archives Canada Cataloguing in Publication

Identifiers: ISBN (softcover): 978-1-7779087-4-4
            ISBN (ebook): 978-1-7779087-5-1

Contents

– That Isn't You – *p.ix*

    – ... in a garden of broken cars – *p.5*

– Why are you here ... – p.7
– The Knowing Tree – *p.9*
– When I Was a Boy Before Watches – *p.11*
– The Halcyon Days – *p.12*
– Lying in Bed and Wondering – *p.13*
– One Morning after the Kill – *p.15*
– Naming the Cats – *p.17*
– I Used to Weed My Mother's Garden After the Rain in Despair – *p.19*
– In a Garden of Broken Cars – *p.21*
– In Different Houses – *p.23*
– Cruel, oh cruel – what lesson did I learn – *p.25*
– on the hilltop at the end of day ... – *p.27*
– Tip – *p.29*
– Awakening – *p.31*
– As the Children Begin to Sing – *p.32*
– Gender Wars of the 1950s – *p.34*
– Canada Day – *p.35*
– The Careful Mind – *p.37*
– Oh How I Long to Be Grateful and True – *p.39*

    – The Summer at the End of Childhood – *p.41*

– Lost in the Language – *p.43*
– Contemplating Photographs of Childhood – *p.45*
– Adolescentulae at first communion – *p.47*
– Suddenly Coming of Age – *p.48*
– First Heat – *p.49*
– Down There – *p.50*
– Girlie Pictures – *p.51*
– Acedia – *p.53*

- Smoking a Pipe like a Poet: was I ever that young – *p.55*
- Whispering Home – *p.61*
- What Memory Forgets – *p.63*
- Since Last You Looked – *p.64*
- Milkweed Girdles – *p.65*
- For My Grandfather – *p.66*
- When I Can't See You and You Can't See Me – *p.68*

– **Going Back** – *p.69*

- As Well as Well – *p.71*
- Making More – *p.73*
- Make Do – *p.74*
- Little Did I Know – *p.76*
- How Do You Deal with Things That Cannot Be Helped – *p.78*
- An Elegy for the Barns at Leeland Farm – *p.79*
- As it Turns Out – *p.81*
- Last Hurrah – *p.82*
- At Night When Raccoons Come for the Corn Like the Knowledge of Eve – *p.84*
- What is it the Spirit Sees When the Body that Holds it isn't There – *p.86*
- The Thousand Tears – *p.89*
- Ode on Homemade Wine at Christmas – *p.91*
- The Physics of Memory, the Mechanics of Dream – *p.92*
- What Holds Us When We're Gone – *p.93*
- Vinegar on the lips of the Lord – *p.95*
- What Can You See When It's Gone – *p.97*
- Renovation – *p.99*
- The Conversation – *p.100*
- Bereft – *p.103*
- Afterword: *Richard (Tai) Grove* – *p.104*
- Author Bio – *p.105*

That Isn't You

The title for **That Isn't You** *is inspired by a comment made by my mother concerning a video transcribed from an old eight-millimeter film. In a still shot, isolated from a single frame of the moving picture, I am riding high on my uncle John's shoulders. When Mother saw the photograph she said "that isn't you," meaning she could not imagine a day from the past when I would have had that kind of relationship with my father's elder brother, the bachelor farmer who lived in our house.*

In the photograph I am obviously delighted and thrilled and full with the joy of riding high on my six-foot-two uncle's shoulders. So, her phrase got me to thinking about "identity" and how we see ourselves, how we are seen by others who might claim to know us well, how we are seen by friends and familiars, how we are seen by strangers, both in chance meetings, and in brief encounters, how we are seen after we pass away when the living refuse to acknowledge what I call 'the full grumble of the dear departed." The true self, the persona, the disconnection between the masks we so often wear to show the world what we wish to reveal, and the face behind the mask. As an aging man I sometimes feel I shave a stranger every morning. I catch a glimpse of my own reflection and wonder, "Who are you?" I was once startled beyond words by being greeted at a family picnic by a seldom-seen relative, "So, how is my sexy cousin doing?" Surely, she could not mean yours truly. It was quite embarrassing because I think she thought I saw myself that way, when it could never be further from the truth.

poems from That Isn't You have appeared in Envoi, an anthology of poems on identity, 101 Portraits, Phantom Parade and the poem "Tip" won the 2021 ($1000 American) Angela Consolo Mankiewicz Poetry Award

dedicated to my love Cathy who knows me …

"Know, first, who you are, and then adorn yourself accordingly."
—*Epictetus*

... in a garden of broken cars

Why are you here …

some future boy
is standing at the closed shut gate
of a graveyard yet to be
clutching a nosegay
of cut chrysanthemums
severed at the stem
in honour of the death of light
his shadow stains
the creak of yawning hinges
like a patina of dust
his life in *this*
the ash the fire leaves behind
as darkness greys
in fading
his flowers stink
of old clothing, of laundry
yet to do
beyond the dry-stone wall
beneath the rubble
of unwritten lives
an estuary of unknown
rivers wait in heaps
like frost heave working
in the winter of the earth
thus moraines pushed by ice
begin to crawl and melt
or foothill scree
comes shivering down a slope
too steep to hold
the heights
and there
beneath the green amnesia
of forgetful grass
the bones of them that took
the discontinued path
reach out with loss of reach
like thirst in shovel-broken roots

those disarticulated hands
all free of final prayer
take up a second purpose
in a gritty glove of sand and soil

why are you here

the question rises
in a smoky whisper
smouldering up as fog
within a patch of warming ground
and 'who are you
as yet to be a *were*'

go find your name
as chiseled smooth
beneath the lichen-blunted
artistry of time
lie here
beside the hero in the pan
how often have I seen
your cities burnt
by breath on mirrors
in the blank museums of the heart
become the winking of a dying star
within the blackness of a troubled eye

The Knowing Tree

at first the fruit
of the knowing tree
comes hard to the hand
an ornament, a bobble
a small taw, a pit, a pebble, a rock
a stone …
then it's a difficult pluck
like pulling the stem
of a cheap pocket watch
wondering what's the hour, what's the day
you've waited out the fragrant buzz
the white wedding
the late-in-the-season frost
that candies the grass
on slow-bee mornings
oh the perfumed dusk
oh the odorous dark

and then the less redolent breezes
come warm to the lassitude of summer
transfiguring the branches
and the cane
those party favours
hung by a busy crew
the orchard fairies
in the brilliant gymnasia of the night
where the green pear dances
flexing its lump
while the rain slips through
like tears
on an apple-cheeked child
and then
begins the great softening
like moon mist

the plum
become a split-skin
sorrowful sweet
reminder
to the cloudy nimbus
of fruit flies
in the bruised spoil
of a kitchen bowl
something the still life
artist might aspire to
were he
to let his brush grow dry
with its tip to the canvas

and were I to think
of the wintering spies
of my childhood
given over
to the memorable espionage
of the farmhouse basement
sagging down
on themselves like cider mash
staining the bent balsa
of a bushel basket
would I see myself in this
the flavour of old February
the taste in the passage of time

When I Was a Boy Before Watches

when I was a boy before watches
before that first jackknife
closed shut in my pocket
as a cut-cotton dullness held
next to my thigh
when time was a mystery
of lost winter mornings
melting away into spring
and summers came
to the let-out of trousers with straw in the cuff
and every anonymous thing
came nameless to life
in the yard and the garden
my smooth cheek
sandpapered by father's be-whisker
in the unshaved evening of the parlour at home
when all but the light
was immortal
at the dying down of the day
though even the star-startled darkness
passed into blue
if I carried the milk
halfway to the house
it was set down twice
for learning the weight
and the strength of my arms
and the ache of it all
white foaming and creamy
and slow and when it was over
the thirst of the moment returned

The Halcyon Days

how many years have passed
since you ran around the house
racing through the parlour
in nothing but your all together
or dressed for morning
only in your pouchy underpants
winking at the fold
when you were boy-breasted
joyfully swimming in your skivvies
shivering at the lake edge
in the white vanish
of wet cotton
dimpled inward at the gusset
like an apple bruise
shall we call those
the halcyon days
before the slow mortification
that widens the hips
and swells the body
with the sanguinary ache
of a new interest
a feathering of secrets
what quickens the pulse points
with perfume
or gives a cherry gloss
to the vermillion border
a sweet flavour to the kiss
black lashes blinking through smoke
as life is threaded through
with the passing of time
like the river that carries the rain
with what we imagine
and what we remember
like aquifers deep in the earth
slaking the wells
and lifting the lakes
like a blue-day mirror
or a looking glass moon with the passing of night
as a stone disappears in the snow

Lying in Bed and Wondering

when I was a boy
lying in a bed of wonder
under the eternal mystery
of a farm-dark sky
I found myself wanting to know
what all the girls in the world
were doing at that exact moment

the ones I knew and
the ones who were strangers
in daylight and strangers at midnight
in obi-synched silk kimonos
or in serapes
washing their hair
in the sacred rivers of distant lands
or walking dust roads
come home under water jugs
filled at a common well

what I knew of the goat-girl
Heidi, or of Becky Thatcher
or of tomboy Scout of Mockingbird
or Helen of Troy, or
Eve of Eden, or Eurydice – she of the bitten heel
lost forever in a land of shadows

I looked for in my sister
my cousins, my school friends
my aunts, my mother
doyens at church, old Annie
waddling down the aisle to the communion rail
blind Mrs. Howell eyes open to darkness in prayer
Crabby Appleton the lady of the horse chestnut tree
hiding from rumours of madness
in the green and prickly pericarps of main street of the village
Mrs. Hardy whose husband loved her
till the day she was stolen
away by time

and the great sadness
that comes to the living
who live on after the dying of love
and I am still-and-forever to this day first-dog
lonely in remembering loss

but if I play
the water in circles of recollection
making waves with my hand full of pebbles
or if I broadcast
the clover
like the feeding of hens in a field
then I watch the dimpled surface of the lake
responding as it would
to the coming of rain
or then I wait
for the season
that feathers the loam
come out of spring and into late summer

I know what breaks the earth open
lifting green life to the sky

or that penny-dross gravel
plunging down where it's chummed
as it shoals in the sand wishes
on the bed of the bay

both somehow the same
as falling *is* rising
to rain on the river
or the sun in a cloud as the river goes dry

One Morning after the Kill

I remember one morning
coming into the kitchen after the kill
as a boy about five
seeing where my grandmother
sat at the table
scalding the pins
from where they were pimpled
in the flesh
and she was foxing the feathers away
in the ambient fragrance of steam
rubbing the hen as it molted
in the wet white heat
rising from the board
and she was garlanded to the wrist
in her work an angel half-born
as she plucked what remained
in the almost rancid smell of warm water
like a pillow left to rot in the rain
and the black that bled
in the soaked newspaper
spread out in the splay
smelled of camphor in ink
and the last ephemeral events
of yesterday's town
blurred as though scorched at the edges
and drifting away on the wind

and then we knew
how Sunday would come
in the roasting aromas of poultry
in the pan
and Monday with dumplings
and Wednesday with thin-meat in soup

and the wishbone
pegged to cure on the pipes of the heater
for my sister and me
we might cheat with our thumbs
for the fracture of faith in good luck
that brittle surprise hackling up in the air
like a green break in time
where the past and the future conjoin

Naming the Cats

the cats on our farm
were all of them barn cats
a wild clowder
of distempered clapperdudgeons
unloved runaways, drop-offs
some blinded in tomcat brawls
some torn-eared ratters, alpha males
weeping yellow matter
in green-eyed midnights
shining down from mow beams
yowling on feed sacks
and mumbling mice
where the gnaw-holes yawned
like ghost mouths in the whitewashed walls
or coming web-whiskered
from windowsills and
sometimes dying
in the crawlspace
under the el of the house
leaving sad verandahs
wool-tagged with sharp-ribbed corpses
lost in leaf shrouds until spring
and out of the mow
cat mothers carried their young
nipped by the neck
scruffing them out and out
among the last lost generation
while anonymous winter
melted into nameless spring
then an unnamed summer
easing into leaf-fallen seasons
that rattle trees naked in the night
oak weather creaking in bone-shadow darkness
like great ships run aground
and wrecked in the yard

and then came the boy
like Adam
given God's purpose
in the cattle pen
and he gave them their names
Whitney Kelly — is that you
and Rock Russell, and
Blackie Lafarge, and Müller
and Graymalkin, El Muerte
and Kemmerick's Boots, and
he loved them all
those raggle-taggle-okey-doke gypsies
he tamed them and
suffered every loss

and if he thought for a moment
about the cat skeleton
in the glass case
at school
the delicate fine-boned posture
of that
frozen-in-motion feline
if he studied
the memory creature in form
as though it were built
from a kit
marked *metaphysics*
what might he learn
or have learned
for there's a fire
that never goes out
till it does
and a flame you can't see
though it's lit from within

I Used to Weed My Mother's Garden After the Rain in Despair

my neighbour
sitting cross-legged on her pebble driveway
looking much the same way
as my sister
playing ball and jacks
with her girlfriend Shirley
timing the bounces
and counting the small swiftness
of metallic stars caught up in her hand
the bounty
like hard seed you might catch
in the palm
when you walk waist deep
through the gone-dry ditches of summer

and this woman
who lives next door
is there at squat in the difficult lotus
methodically weeding the gravel
with the studied precision
of an archeological dig
she tugs at what creeps
at what sets its root
deeper than rain
so that when she pulls
the sharp-grained rock
spills backward in heaps
of grey dross
like the shedding of eskers
leaving a patch
clean-stoned in her wake
this being – in the hopefulness of her suburban mind
the end-row ennui of a life-free zone

nothing to leap out at the edge of the grass
nothing to live in the sun
no lion-toothed nor broadleaf weed
to worry the sky
when darkness falls there
like the flat of the hand
on a field mouse, no wild interloping of hares
nor a fox kit running home
in the gloaming
caught in a veil of tree-sheltered moonlight

and she toils for an hour
edging backwards on the ache of her rump
as though in retreat from the shores of the sea
as it ebbs for the thing she is doing
is like dream work
when the moonlight she's dreaming turns green

In a Garden of Broken Cars

title taken from a line in the novel Unsheltered *by Barbara Kingsolver*

> *lost in memory like words into thoughts*
> *after listening*
> *I recall how ...*
>   JBL

my uncle lived on sandy land
the soil as soft and fine
and pie flour
a sift of powdered alluvium
that puffed up
from billowing underfoot
upon the beige breath of our passing
sent forth in whirls of dust
while out in the yard
he kept a garden of broken cars
where tracing their wings on glass
a rage of wasps
danced in the terpsichorean heat
rehearsing anger
in the glazier's apiary
where they hived
coming out of old upholstery
stinging the windshield
from within a buzzing choreography
and dropping down through the floorboards
upon the hot skillet of the land
like a sinful swarm of prideful angels
and there
on the hail-blackened acres
of a bruise-leafed crop
weathered by the penury
of a bad-luck summer

we played
in the automobile graveyard
in that static energy
of oil-redolent time-seized engines
dreaming of back roads
and tar-fragrant pavement
coming from somewhere
other than somewhere else
those jalopies their odometers
having clicked over one last inch
till they sank on their wheels where they stayed
in the four dry ruts
like the ghostly journey
on a mile map
of a felt-tip pen
tracing lines that vanish beyond themselves

In Different Houses

it was so different to be
in different houses
in the Simpson home
where I spent a week as a child
rich with its woodsmoke smells
lingering even in laundered
hand-me-down blue
button-collared shirt
I once wore
the fragrance of sunlight
and Borax
blent with clean split-cedar
kindling burned into the fabric
the sweet sting
of that cold fire would not wash away
perfuming even the threaded pearl
that held like mother thumbs about the heart
and over the pulse points
of the blue-river wrists
that redolence of youth
lacing the mind
with a permanent touch
like the feel of a pinch
or an itch
out of reach
the caressing by cloth
of a breath taken in
and released
and where am I now
and where was I then
lost in the vagabond hour
with its failure to stay
like the wind
that skips on a wave
that shirt that my cousin outgrew
came to my shoulders
like smoke on the smouldering bone of a branch

and then it was gone
in a year
with a brother nowhere
in the world as an heir
it was torn
like a weed from the earth
indifferent houses
that empty their rooms
when the darkness won't shelter the day

Cruel, oh cruel — what lesson did I learn

in the parental penum of my youth
I suffered
the deprivation of counting the lash
of the slat of the blind
on the sash
above the frost-feathered panes
framed by mullions
in the half darkness
and having been sent to bed
hungry in the last afternoon hours
of bedroom isolation
with winter's witchery
of branches scratching at the window
like skeletal fingers
clawing the blear from under the ice
and the cold dust bloomed
in frothy tumbles over linoleum
waxed to a yellow sheen
glazing fake chrysanthemums
shining like smoker's china
and in the punitive solitude
of that boreal house
I waited
for the slow-clock execution
of evening
and the seconds and the minutes and the hours
dripped down
as they wept and grew
like fangs from the eaves
stalactites of ice on the broken-bone jaw
of a great and beastly
incarceration

locked in the living leviathan of night
that swallowed the moon
in veils of mist
and all the light-sustaining stars
winked like embers dying into the black cloak
of a sky-fallen world
and I slept away
the darkness
until now ...

... and yet behind closed eyes I see him waiting on the top of the hill at the end of the day ...

our farm dog Tip
would come wilding up
out of the ditch
when cars came
interloping along the road
from the village
a mile away to the east
and it seemed
there was no way of curing him
of that need he had
though he'd be struck
and sent tumbling
like mud from the wheel
you'd see him
from the hilltop
sometimes coming home
half-broken
kicking up land
little whirls of dust in his wake
like a visible twist
in the breath of weather
and it was loving him
that made me
lock him up
as you might a wayward child
it was love
that made me
wish he weren't
wolf dreaming
and moonlit

I want an ancient fire
to keep him close
but memory
is a long-roped sorrow
and earth burns
what is sky lost
with the shadow vanish of autumn
and the smouldering shade
that stinks of darkness
in the slow extinguishment of scorched rain

Tip

my first dog Tip died in the dark
lying alone on the floor at the barn
his body gone hard
in the cold of the night
like a branch that broke off at the graft
and then broke again
as it fell to the earth
where he lay in the curl of himself
among chop sacks and
snap-string hay
in the fragrance of silage
of rolled oats and molasses
and wheat straw
shook of its dust
and whitewash rubbed
from the rock as with each white stone
you might think of the full moon
coated in mist

and the cruel gods
brought the news to the house
in the snow
blown in at the door
and oh my slow-to-wake heart
you'd think it might
be inured to death
and dying
accustomed as I was by then
to failing runts and scouring calves
and distempered cats
their eyes sewn shut
by the green weep of crusted suppuration

but in truth
I suffered every loss
even that of the old ewe
her last fleece
tattered at her shoulder
like the torn-away sleeve
of a mendicant's coat
even she
who snuffled to breathe
the yellow snooze
worming her nostril
and not-at-all beautiful
come and go
with an effluent
flux of her lungs

her lamb twins leaping
as I might leap
in the milk-breath of morning
to think of my mother
as young
and my first dog Tip
a fat pup calling joy out of sorrow
and sorrow from joy

Awakening

I was a boy sleeping in the den
on the hard leather
of the oak-slat couch
under the sepia-tone
photographs of my ancestors
their ghost faces glowing grey
in gold-gild frames
as they had all
died into the light they were born from
like the cold fog
of a winter garden
come into spring
my young mind haunted
by the gravity of their lives
gone in that door-closed room
but for the brass
and silver and all
the Royal ribbons
garlanding the glass
of the high-top desk
all the time-tarnished
glory of the farm …
and I was there
in the night
visited by an awakening
a strange and awestruck
stirring like a lamb dropped in the straw
come April at the barn
in the full wonder of new life

how like rain on the house
the shiver that comes with sinning

As the Children Begin to Sing

when we were children
one of our games involved
us playacting
in the upstairs hallway
pretending to walk the aisle
singing a mock version
of *the wedding song*
from Wagner's Lohengrin

> *here comes the bride*
> *big fat and wide*
> *here comes the groo-oom*
> *skinny as a broom*

my sister and cousins
joining in
as something of a thumbsucker
choir in chorus

and with a tattered veil
smouldering in white
fogging along the floor
like the ghost smoke
of dying fire
and we stood by the bookcase
taking our vows
lost in the trip-shadow
of time
when time takes on shape
of memory
as breath on words
made visible in winter

and what imaginary widow
lets go my arm
as I slip away
like something adrift
a leaf perhaps
in the faith loss of autumn
in movement toward imaginary spring

and my mother
after spousal death
laments her greatest sorrow
as being
that of not having someone
to do nothing with

and I see them
together in the parlour
listening to the quiet
in the comfort of companionable silence

as the children begin to sing

Gender Wars of the 1950s

my sister had a *Betsy Wetsy* doll
a bald-headed rubber infant
with blue eyes and a perfect
bore hole for a mouth
and a complimentary
circle cut in the body between the legs
it came with a small
squeeze bottle
affixed with a nipple that fit the face
squeeze the liquid from the bottle
then squeeze the belly of the doll
and thus the faux baby
watered the world with a wet completion
well to tap, tap to bottle
bottle to doll, doll
to diaper, diaper to potty
potty to sink, sink to drain
drain to tile bed weeping into the lawn
where the grass grew
as with one wet expression of ultra green
and me with my cap gun
a red paper spool of small explosions
hiding behind the door
seeking the chemical sting
and the stink of burn
firing freely
as with each smoky bang
I killed the breath of the black-hat world
my sister coddled and cradled
and cooed to sleep her little trust
while I gave villains their due
with what emptied the room
and broke the chairs to kindling
in a splintering darkness of the mind
from arm to fist, fist to finger
finger to trigger, trigger to muzzle, muzzle
to grave
and whisky all round for the thirsty dead

Canada Day

Father: "I live in the greatest country in the world."
Son: "Dad, how would you know, you've never lived anywhere else?"

when I was a boy
given to dreaming
as we drove along
the Bluewater Highway
going west to Mooretown
I found myself
looking over the way
across the river
at the long green lawns
of alien America
knowing how for generations
my family
was fecund with a sanguinary
connection like sunset gone crimson on water
with radiant roots
flung wide and wild as kite strings
cut loose and casting their thread shadows
on that foreign land
think of fishing line leaded for sinking
and beaded with tears from the river
I felt the strange pull of invisible lives
as though in the shoaling of souls
laid to rest
in the earth far away
from my home
a rising of spirits
like fog out of stone grown cold
in the grey-green hollows
of occupied time

and my father
following the black flow of macadam
holding his middle name true
to the light
that falls on the ink
by the slant of the hand
or the stain on the page
what it says of himself
it also says of me
for what the mirror catches
by distance refused
and what the eye
plans for the mind
in the foreground
are lost in past promise
with a voice
in the fold of a book
and his life
at the source
like a long-ago vanishing star

The Careful Mind

if I were to say of myself
in the hope of knowing
myself I might say
of myself that mine
has ever been a careful mind

when I was a child
I had a notion
that someday I might
become a most generous
of all greengrocers
giving my wares away
so the least of the village children
need not steal
as it was when one
particularly light-fingered girl
was caught
with her candy sack full
and the stain of her shame
like grass-green knees
or the black-tongued glory
of licorice
licked down to the corneal white
of what was
marbled within
the anise of a coal-voiced
word so sweet in the saying
it seemed to slither away
in a serpentine hiss
but she for recompense
was struck
on her bike by a car
so she flew
through the air
like a branch snapped clean in a storm

and the surgeons
shaved her scalp and
knitted her bone
that had fractured about her brain
like the rind of a gourd
left to rot
in a gone-to-seed garden

and that left me
tracing a line
like a slow-fingered child
with a difficult book
or the nail that follows the river's
blue ink on a page
the ragged coast
of the land by the ocean
cragged and crooked as the savage edge
of wind-ripped water

and the moral bargain
of the pure soul
at the centre of stone
where a widow
lay a fingertip kiss
like a droplet of rain
on a lost-to-life name

what I learned
of the full-of-care mind
like a man
with his pockets pulled out
for want of a coin
to become he who dreams of a day
when the dreaming is free

Oh How I Long to Be Grateful and True

if you know what it means
to feel sad without sorrow
or what it is
to weep without grief
if you remember
in childhood
how you suffered
the seemingly ineluctable hurt
of an unswallowable sob
lodged in the throat like a stone
how it always passed in woeful
peristalsis melting away
in a soluble lump
like the sugar that sweetens warm tea

how life as a blow
to the back
from a fall
might make you wish to say

I cannot catch my breath

though your breath
was only briefly stolen
like the silence in ink
where you lay on the earth
while the apples remained in the tree

and that
melancholia
of the naughty daughter
and that of the disobedient boy
comes on strong
as ice is strong
until it thins
over waves, thins
at a stream, thins

in the middle out far
where the cold sun
brightens and burns a blue seam
like a weld in weak steel

there where the blind fox
drowns, there
where the heart of the sailor
goes still
in the deep responding of sand
to an anchor, sand
to a broken-rope man

who builds a life
out of durable loss
enduring the orphans of Auschwitz
enduring the Hibakusha of Hiroshima
enduring the fate of the vanishing islands
and the displaced and the diaspora
oh war-torn Syria, oh refugees of Yemen

and me

now my mother's a gull in the air
and my father's a hawk in blue sky
and I've a loving of friends
who aren't there at all
when the heavens are vacant with flight …

oh, how I long
to be grateful and true

as my ancestors crossed
the wide fever
come over the dark light-starved waters
arriving here in this land of endless winter
where wolf shadows darken deep snow

... the summer at the end of childhood

Lost in the Language

"... the intention has always been to produce a living, inclusive and readable piece of work ... In other words, the ambition has been 'poetry'."

from Simon Armitage's introduction to his translation of 'Sir Gawain and the Green Knight

... if I am lost
in the outdoor language
of children and farmers
where the wet tongue plays loose
with the taste of each word
and the fragrance
of fresh-fallen rain
comes alive as it rises from the sun-burned pavement
where footfalls
touch the stain of the shade in retreat
of evaporate waters

we are drawn by the eye to the natural blue
where the day moon
hangs and is sand-dollar white
with its purchase of heaven
come out of the sea

I want when I walk
into birdsong
some of it lovely, some of it
raw as a wound
as I enter the sexual chorus of spring
if not for redwing screeching from a reed standing stiff
as a rod thrust deep in the mud of the swale
with its peeper-frog chorus
abrupted by the deep-throated burp of one grandfather frog

what rots at the root
or greens at the tip
is piercing the mirror both ways
where it laid its reflections
full out
like an arrow that misses its mark

and what
of the verdant reply
in the wind-quiver
palm of a not-quite-gathering hand

if I consider
the nakedness longing
in me to describe
where in the timeless Eden
of the wild
or on the fallen world of the farm
life's there in the flesh
like the muck on the belly
the muck on the shell
and the muck as a mask on the spirit of stone

Contemplating Photographs of Childhood

it was a time
when we were green as Eden
in the mind
our bodies small
we colted through the yard
like lambs we leapt
on slim legs
jolting as we raced and climbed
up wagon racks
and corncrib fences
mow laddered in the rafters of the barn
we cooed as pigeons coo

and we were silk on corn
or milkweed sap
lactating at bend of stem
our seed-kites formed within a purse
hay sweet
and soft as gluten-gum
we blew about
like chaff in breath
or shook like pocket silver
in a hand count stopped at ten

melting all our worth in sleep
we dreamed ourselves
come naked in the touch of rain
bay-watered to the heart
we caught our breath
in shivers wading through
white sleeved with tan
we danced our flat palms
rocked by waves
to catch us flying
as geese might land at end of day

and as our mischief
settled into grey-faced photographs
the slow emulsion
of a darkness come too soon
to fog our youth
we lost the vigor of our innocence
and sought
another paradise
where flowers ache in bloom
like catch of flame
and shadows drop through
deep wood branches
of an inner wilderness

Adolescentulae at first communion

In white gloves
and lacy skirts the colour of milk
the young girls
come to the altar
kneeling in supplication
for want of first communion
tasting the bread and
drinking the wine
of the flesh and the blood of Christ
atoning for original sin of virginal Eve
who upon tasting the fruit
of the tree of knowledge
of good and evil
saw that she was naked
her body shining
like polished marble
in the statuary of ancient Rome
her sense of herself as softly blooming
blushing with life
and the sudden awareness
of the shadows that veil us all

The Summer at the End of Childhood

Twas the summer of the end
of childhood
the year she came to the river
shocking us all
in her two-piece swimsuit
stepping out on the pier
umbilicus-beautiful
as though from the time
of that first maternal unbuttoning
that day
with dock stones
sharp in the sole of the foot
and the soft tar
hot to the touch
so it smeared the palms of our hands
to grip the ladder
where the fragrance of bitumen
blent with the chemical stink
of the river St. Clair
blooming blue like heaven
fallen before us
receiving us all
as though in fluvial baptism
a sacred second holy ablution
of the body
sunk to the heartbeat
and pulse points
in an aqueous caress
of liquefied darkness cooling the flesh
from within
where soul is said to reside
like oil in a cruet
the way it tips to be seen in a glass
as an ointment anointing the light
we're favoured by

Suddenly Coming of Age

we'd been children playing scrub
all afternoon
when, in the dying of the day
we walked across the graveled-grass gloaming
moving west over sheep droppings
and sap-fragrant windfalls strolling toward the house
when one of the girls in the game
as though suddenly coming of age
casually shone the weakening beam
of a low-lux torch
so it cast a dim amber circle
the shape of the mouth of a jar
a pale-water moon
a luminous lamping of the seam of her shorts
the relief of her genital fold like an in-breath of denim
and she mimed first heat by humping the light
the mocking menarche of her rut
insisting she prove herself human
the cider-sap scent of the apples
high on the breath of the yard
as we wandered through time
as though we weren't anyone's children
though she was a daughter of Eve
with a wound the shape of a heart
where the heart drops down through the body
like ripening fruit with its stem given way
to the feathering pull of the earth

First Heat

when adolescence made me shy of girls
as dogs are sometimes
shy of guns — my will to wish gone
tuck tail hiding in the gorse
at first report of powder on the wind
and yet I found myself pursued
like sunlight chasing shadows
in the shade — I went away
to seek a sleeper's safe dishabille
or off to find a bather's body
lounging in the waterline
where soap betrays a shining knee
emerging from the grey circumference
as islands
in the moon tide
slip a liquid noose
upon a bony archipelago
of rocks revealed
as they were once in deeps concealed
how then
the dreamer's heart
might lift a secret rumour in the breast
like raindrops on a droughty stem
the dry earth thirsting in the night
a petal in a web of dew
a trace of tears that soak the secret
of the flesh
where we might hear
the *still small voice*
between the apple and
the hand
what bends the bough in slow release
become the letting go of things received
like coins of thought that drop their golden burden
when they're spent

Down There

when we were young at the lake
sometimes we would swim in our skivvies
we innocent playmates
disrobed on the beach
stripped down
to our briefs and panties
white cotton that vanished
if it clung to wet flesh
though ballooning behind
swollen with water
and sand
burbled and burped
to be struck with a squirt
by the palm of the hand
and you couldn't help see down in front where girls
folded inward on fabric like petals
or boys gathered in appley lumps
our gender revealing itself
to the sweet seduction of waves that sat us down fast
with a slap and a suck
where we tumbled and rolled
like the schooling of fish
in the silver relief of the sun
on the shoaling of pebbles and shells of the shore
and our separate bodies aware they were bodies
also knew how it tingled *down there*
where the lure of the undertow
felt like the dark draw of a sweet caress
from deep in the lake
where you'd drown in desire
if you ever stepped in *stepped in stepped all the way in*

Girlie Pictures

in my best friend's basement
at the back of a pressed-oak roll-top desk
in a small locked drawer
clicked with a key so delicate
it seemed like a sliver of metal
you might pluck or brush from the bed of a lathe
and there, concealed under a single sheet of split balsa
fragrant with soap and perfumed wax
used to ease it in sliding
tucked away in the bottom
like adult espionage
we found the well-thumbed
magazine
something forbidden to children
a series of black & white
photographs of girls and women
posing in the nude
their flesh grey
as emolument
taking on the salacious sheen
of fixed images
lifted from emulsion and pinned up
to dry in a pornographer's darkroom
skivvies on a wash-line
frillies in the wind
these are something, these were much
but to see what the man upstairs
my best friend's father (a spy in the house of love)
kept hidden away
in Rosicrucian shadows
surely he must never know
how his only son and I snuck a peek
before returning the evidence of our sinning
to its hiding place
but oh how our young hearts
doing springtime lover's double dutch
set to skipping in our chests

Acedia

I am listening to the listlessness
of CBC radio
when the wise professor
comes on
and gives us all in mid pandemic
the gift of the word *acedia*
that monastic melancholia
of noon-hour torpor
that sets in
like the smoke that stains
the soul when the soul
dies down to a spark of darkness
he says it with a hard C
grieving the full ache
of that consonant
that cat cough of the alphabet
the one abecedarians
hack in hard sentences
and the academic
understands how the sun
slows down to shadow loss
perched in the blue zenith
of mid day

and I think of those childhood Sundays
when I entered
the ennui
of enervated hours
with nothing to do
one sorrowful moment
in the snow dial
of a February oak
each branch coursing the yard
like the bony finger
of a deciduous witch etching
steely ephemera of wintering earth

and what am I describing
mid scratch
my pencil in movement
over the page
catching a breath of meaning
as a spider web
with its deathwatch mistress
reads the final anguish
of a mayfly
the lady harpist
of windowsill and dew
the threadbare sorrow throbbing in her mind
like a silent harp

Smoking a Pipe like a Poet:
was I ever that young

"I always saw it as sitting upstairs, smoking a pipe like a poet."
Paul McCartney

i

when my Aunt Stella
came in the car to our house
to visit the farm
from the city
I'd accompany my father
for she didn't drive
I'd sit in the back while she smoked
all the way home
lost there in the blue fog
of the automobile
barely able to breathe
my young lungs
locked in that winter aquarium
gasping for air
and squinting through the sting
of that withering wisp
of a burning cigarette
set in the ashtray
like incense abandoned
or candle snuff
the way the fragrance
of an extinguished wick
can fill a church
entire
in an instant expiration of the flame
the way smoke whispers
like a breath in cool air
unraveling above the altar
with the redolence of perfumed wax
refusing the fire

and I loved my aunt
as she sat
chattering beside my father
both of them ghosts now
spirits of the mind
in memory
a conjuring of struck matches
and lipstick filters
crushed in black ashes
small white pillars bent in a cluster
like a vision of sorrow
when the voice of a loved one
goes grey

ii

I stole alone
into the farmhouse kitchen
opened the trash can lid
and pilfered the fag ends
of my aunt's ashtray
plucking them out
one by one
though they were wet
as potato peels and
thus unlikely to burn
I would straighten them
each and all
like the penury
of a poor carpenter
with a palm
full of bent nails
and in the privacy of a corn row
I'd strike a Lucifer's sulfurous stick
and smoke myself dizzy
on the slow draw of a filter

and I wonder
was I ever that young
imagine myself
gone backwards
into the womb
like an in-breath of Eden

iii

my cousin Bill
bought me my first pack
of Rothmans
at Dresden Fair
and I brought them home
with a penny-match package

where I sat in my bedroom
at my makeshift homemade
orange-crate and plywood desk
tapped one from the set
struck fire
and seeing myself seeing myself
placed my hands
on the keys
of an Underwood QWERTY
blinking into the sting
preparing to play
"let the poems begin …"

when my mother
opened the door and came in

me waving the smoke
like a gull wing in fog

and that was the end of the pack

"I won't tell your father"
she said

and I knew
that her silence was wise

and I learned from the quiet of women
and I learned from the weakness of men

iv

in first year university
living in the false tower
of Saugeen-Maitland
in the den of iniquity
an evil on the edge of the campus
I'd purchased
a pack of cigarettes
forgetting to buy matches
and there
in the evening solitude
of my dorm room
I stripped the cellophane
opened the box
pulled out one virgin cigarette
as white to the filter
as new chalk
when it occurred to me
that I had no matches
and so
out of frustration
I tried to draw fire
from the heat in the glass
of an incandescent light bulb
thereby learning
a lesson on the failure of combustion
a foolish frustration

and I thought of the lines
from a Leonard Cohen poem
"if you're the light
buddy
then give me a light"

and there was no one there
but I
and I was a boy
without matches
alone in a room
like a lad on an island
and shipwrecked at sea
on strange sand

v

for a while
I smoked American cigarettes
unfiltered *Pall Mall*
in a soft pack
plucking tobacco from my tongue
the chemical fragrance
of Virginian nicotine and arsenic
and John Rolfe's Caribbean blend

then it was wine-tipped
cigarillos
and a burn-your tongue
blend of *Borkum Riff*
and *Irish Mead*
and the bitter spittle
tapping the pipe stem
till it wept in your palm
and that was the way of it

until I grew tired of coughing
it was five years
of foolishness

a lustrum
of small sinning

"… curse Sir Walter Raleigh
he was such a stupid get …"

and I wonder
was I ever that young

and I think to myself
not yet

Whispering Home

for a time in my youth
I worked at Rondeau Park Point
where the waves crested high
and the lake
roared in on the breakers
while the deep
and resonant voice of the water
surged in dips and hollows
that drew fast at the dangerous shore
while the big blue heaven-coloured
leviathan slipped
and shoaled and sucked
at the pebbled weave
like the cross-thread loom
of a drowning machine
and there
in that powerful
and often exhausted
silver school sunder of tumbling light
frothing with madness
in fossils and shells
and fractured glass
rubbed smooth as though
by the worrying thumbs of God
we waded in and were struck back
with the big stagger
of small creatures
gripping at foam
as we fell aching for breath
like the fall from a branch
of a child grown ripe on the bough

small bird
refused by the wing
and the world on the wind
was a mother-voiced word
wanting us back in the palm of the bay
where the bottom lay sure
in the small of the foot
with a wish
that went whispering *home*

What Memory Forgets

what were we to make
of the heifers at frolic in the field ...
you with your new breasts swelling
like midsummer fruit
and me with desire
straining in the cloth
against my will
two measures of the body
born to nature
while nettles itch against the fences
and thistles
bloom in wool
blue plums would split their skins
and weep before they fell
and all the lazy apples
drum the cider fragrant grass
young hearts of spring grown wild with life
the gorgeous doom of humans
wearing only light
to fret like moody dreamers
aching in the flesh

Since Last You Looked

one minute
we were simply children at play
and she was walking the top rail
instep, instep, turn
with all the aplomb
of an Olympic gymnast
she stopped at a cant in joy
arms out angel form
like a cormorant
drying her wings on a post
one leg extended for performance
and oh she was such
a sky-loved marionette
testing her strings
balanced there to the very limits of her body
until she slipped
and straddled the fence
with the pelvic shock
of a full-weight bifurcation
shuddering along
the whitewashed two-by-six
as even the water set to shivering
in the rain gauge
measured by a trembling
as though cooling from boil
and so we learn
though we're adored for a while
finding ourselves in heaven's favour
then like the midge
that smoulders in a windowsill
like a breath-stirred thread gone still
seeking a way out of the self-burning blackness
that darkens life from within
when what breaks our fall isn't God
but the wolf tooth of the world
cracking the bone for want of the marrow
that sorrows the lamb into silence

Milkweed Girdles

in my youth
even the skinny girls
wore girdles
foundations
rubberized undergarments
meant for holding in
all the flesh that jiggles
thin tummies vulcanized by necessary fashion
and exigent umbilical culture
pinched in by that pliable armour draping garter belt buttons
hanging toward the floor like tatters torn from rags
purposeful tassels fringing the waist
and marking the all-day-Sunday thigh
like the imprint of a hot coin
little women in training bras and
crinoline flaring skirts
that flashed small gill breaths
of their hems in beauty
flaring open above the knee
like peonies in bloom bent double by the weight of rain
and even my sister
and all my female cousins
would wash their hair on Saturday night
then sleep in painful curlers
pricking into the scalp like cockleburs
pressing into heady dreams of the mornings to come
when walking out the door
on wobble heels and stockings
into the wilding wind   into the drench of downfall
and into all the disheveling weathers of the world
where hothouse orchids
misbehave like dew that weeps upon the green
and as with all the storm-torn butterflies
clinging to the floss, these girls
must wait for the sun that comes to set them free then
tossing their wings in flights of far away

For My Grandfather

... after a poem by Don Gutteridge

"You will not always have me with you"

my grandfather said to me
in the small parlour
next to the kitchen
where grandma was busy
clattering away and clearing the dishes
doing the Vestal dance
of wifely women — what passed
for love in the latter days of the sixties
an involvement of aprons
and sensible shoes
and there we were, he and I
amongst antimacassar doilies
that lace toss like oversize snow
the work of tatting and
hair-oil amber like wild carrot
brought in from the fences
in the ditch at the edge of the field
absent the purple prick
at the centre
and throw rugs rucked with walking
he said those sacred words

"You will not always have me with you"

a homily to the spirit
a blessing to the body
spoken as though he weren't there then
as he wouldn't be there much past
the wind shiver of winter
and I at seventeen
in the melancholy midst
of that much-loved man's mortality
while his heart kept faith
until sunlit May came beating over an eastern hill
like a cloth-draped drum
with its slow truth
sounding and sorrowful "you will not always have me with you"
giving breath
to the sad word "gone"

When I Can't See You and You Can't See Me

Though I see you looking
and you're looking at me

I wonder: what do you see
when the room is empty?

You see *nothing* by morning
and *nothing* all night.

Yet you see darkness in darkness
and light in the light.

… going back

As Well as Well

might I not go back through individual time
with a wish
for correcting the days
in recollection
as differing from what I did
or did not do …
meanwhile the brave illusion of each real event
still lingers
like a waking dream
as mist outlasts
the clarifying heat
within the haze
the close horizon of the tree-toothed bay
some days goes lost
for hours in a milky blur
of dampened blue
and yet I know the line
remains a broken comb
of distant life
the lie of sight denies
sometimes the far off hills
beyond the spit of sand
reveal themselves as well
dark heaps of stone
like cattle resting in a field
at night the city glows
against the gloaming sky
and so
is there as well
what's in the murk and stir
is ever present
though it settle back to limpid clarity
what shines the glass

as deep as light will go
in darkness
darkens light to truth
a countless count of stars
a single moon
fox-fragrant evening eloquent and black
while insects sing of nothing   but themselves

Making More

what fills the mind halfway is also
what carries the thirst to the field
in an ice-jangling darkness
an imaginary
shadow-line in the bone of the skull
and the jug that is cold
where the zest floats
and pips drift
and the blur dissolves
within the alternating sour-sweet
supersaturate silting of white sugar
just enough for the touch points
budding on the tongue
with a cool slake
that lightens the heft
of lemon-fragrant well water
as with an ever-so-brief
tipping of the spout
to the mouth

the man lies in grateful reclining
full-out in the rural oasis
of oak shade
at the fence line saying
drink in — oh, drink in
drain the cup
to an absence
there's love sufficient to the kitchen
for making more

Make Do

on the make-do poverty
of the farm
the hired man sat
in the off-kitchen shed
under the chattering hand
of his master, my uncle
the one he called *Red Hocks*
who was shearing his hair
so it was short on the sides
with a thin whisper
breathing on top
like the fire-blackened crozzle of singed
though not-quite-burned-away grass
his grey scalp like a husk
he was a small-headed man
built short to the floor
and this
always seemed
good enough for him
this saving of a quarter
taking the sharp harvest
like April at the barn
with its lugubrious bleating
and the ewe-shiver
and the fleece-fall
and the almost-mournful
maa of new-lamb mothers
lamenting the last of the cold
coming in at the half door

but he wasn't woolled
he wasn't upended and fearful
though he sat
towel-shouldered
and in submission
to this utilitarian trim
the last of it falling
like smoke from a pipe in a downdraft
and we were that poor
for it to be good enough
for a common happiness
to be
thus broomed away
and out the door   running

Little Did I Know

little did I know
that when cattleman
Ken Muth
spent the weekend at our farm
commiserating about
the breed that he and my father
had husbanded
with important results
a line of impressive daughters
sired by our bull Cloudburst
bellowing at the barn
and when I heard this visitor
opine about
the blow sand of his home county
"anyone who tries to tell you
you can grow anything
other than tobacco
on that land
is either a cursed liar or
a damned fool"
meanwhile I listened
hearing only above
the sonorous voices of self-important men
the lowing come to the house
from the meadow
beyond the garden
that mournful ululation
of sorrowing mothers
sounding above the graze
like women in the valleys of Egypt
their hands gored crimson with Biblical sunset
burnt to the colour of blood

never in my boyhood mind
weaned in the corn-rich
wheat-golden loams of my youth
never did it occur to me
that I might one day
build a life away from my childhood home
a hundred miles east along the lake
living in Ken Muth country
in the land of fools and liars
in the bountiful contradiction
where the fertile earth
refuses the kiln
and the shatter-glass greenhouses
have fallen to ruin
like the ghost light of wave-washed ice
glazing the edge of the earth

How Do You Deal with Things That Cannot Be Helped

when my father and I
slept together at the fair
in the bed at the back
of the pickup truck
first we shook out
a bale of new straw
making a nest in the box
laying out a time-worn quilt
for the pricks
in the wheat-scented softness
the yellow reply
of each shaft and stem
piercing the patches
like a blunt needle crafting a new design
sharp elbowed and feckless
and on this old counterpane
we zippered ourselves in
like sleeping-bag larvae
and went wordlessly to sleep

in the morning
emerging like wingless imago
we shaved in cold water
show pails hung from the side mirrors
rinsing our razors
in the foamless chill
and washing our faces
as wildwoods walkers do at a stream

oh how I wish I could go back in time
and say something in the night
to the man in the mirrors or morning
the small soap unseen by himself on his throat
softly rising
the sorrow of it like a ghost
in a whisker of daylight

An Elegy for the Barns at Leeland Farm

how voluptuous
are the whitewashed
fieldstones
of the foundations of the big barn
like the round hips
of full-bodied women
working the earth in a garden
chalked in lime
that almost remembering
of the frost float
of the field at the fences
remembering all
the way we sometimes
remember the cold
rising up from the snow
like horse breath
those stones to be heaved to a boat
and brought here
as an old heaviness of a sorrowful heart
might sob into place
carrying life in a mournful breast
and then to be set there
for the dry wall mason's
expert approval at
the hitching away of a vanishing view

to stay there then
a hundred years
in the oak-beam darkness
until with a final
subsidence time slid down
in a sandy scree
and the gravel sank in at the shoulders
like a grave in an untended yard

O look to the hill
where the ghost of those buildings
calls out to the blue-raftered moon
there's a dog
at a kind man's fire
with a wolf in his dream
running slow

As it Turns Out

as it turns out
time has been
smoking at the barn
dropping its match in the hay
a smouldering
like fog above a grave
read there
the names of fire written
in flame
leaping out at your feet
what licks the rafters
like a horse
after salt in old wood
is daylight
come down from a knothole
swirling in shafts
of luminous dust
like a birthing of moths
burning their wings
in gold wheat
see Chronos
he stands by the silo in shade
tapping the ash from his pipe
on his heel
his embering hours
given over to heat
at the centre of stone
as grandfather gathers his shadow
where darkness is rucking its cloth

how clean is the hill
without buildings
where each rock like a pit in a peach
is thinking of leaving the land
not as flame
might leap from a branch
no more like fire gone deep
as the heart of a man gone still in the earth

Last Hurrah

deep in the dark recesses
of the basement
I remain in redolence of wet leather
and the salt stink
of manly exertion
the fragrance
of winter lingers
as it occupies the scarecrow shape
of the hockey tree
like the skeletal presence
of a stripped-to-the-bone player
and I am that
skinflint homunculus
emptied onto crossed sticks
my skates
hung blades to the ceiling
boots to the floor
a pouring out slow
of blackstrap shadow
from a foot-shaped vase
and there I am
the odour in the dark
the ghoul's perfume
that soaks the cellar
like the rumour of someone lurking
long after childhood's
last hurrah

if you sniff this poem
take a deep inbreath
like a dog
at the crack of a door
what seeps off the page
impregnating these inky word smells
I am with you
like the exhaustion of wishes
withering in candle smoke
the soul of your lost father
and vinegar
that apples cold earth

At Night When Raccoons Come for the Corn Like the Knowledge of Eve

think of the sweet corn
silkening night on the farm
when the polecats came
thieving, breaking the green
so the wet sap weeps
at the fracture, the bent-double stalk
like a child's bone
wounded by falling
and those small hands
those almost human hands
peeling the satiny husk
with that fine hair
spilling out at the tip of the cob
each strand of silk like a thread licked twice
for mending
that larcenous hunger
of moonlit sinners
grown fat in the luminous dark
while we sleep
and think of the earth
where the root work held
like a hen's foot scratching for stone
look there
to the labouring soil
where life grips
and drinks at the dippering care
drawn in sips from the well
while the housewife's work
lies half-eaten on the once-watered soil of her garden

that rabble, those ruffians
lay waste the much pampered crop
like worms and smut
and weed and heat
and drought and hail
come bruising with blight
on black blemished leaves
in the big-bellied winds of a storm
that cut through the field
in a swath
that might level the land
that it came for

come morning
bring on your brilliant mask of light
with its blue knowledge of heaven
and nothing to harvest
and nothing to show for your labour
but beauty and beauty's divine and invisible twin

What is it the Spirit Sees When the Body that Holds it isn't There

anhydrous ammonia wept
from the end-of-the-row nozzles
white tears
like milk from the teats
of a cow who needs milking
dripping in dust

my uncle
climbed down from where
he'd been ringing the empty drum of the sprayer
with the wet clang
of a measuring stick
the damp tip a dark inch
from the need to return to the source
with the corn spiked green in the sun
as though from drought

why am I thinking
of my sister
her hair tied up
in butterflies of stained paper
meant for dyeing herself at home
sitting in a chair in the kitchen
patiently waiting for the imagined beauty
of a cheap chemical perm
to take its time at transformation
of shape and colour

as though this were the body of a dream
I can't wake from
I think also of ammonium nitrate
stored in the stale harbour of Beirut
suddenly exploding
as it has grown unstable
as it will when it is forgotten
by bad governance and incompetent corruption
seized cargo that levels the city
leaving one wall standing
in the midst of rubble
like a monolith on the surface of the moon

and one horrible moment
the fertilizer
hissing in his face
my uncle took the pressurized
vapour where it exhausted itself
like the last breath of a great mechanical beast

and for weeks
he was blinded
his cheeks puffed crimson
with the toxic sting
the flesh peeled
like red lacquer
leaving a pale dermis
bleached and raw
he sat at the table
as though he'd been burned in the war

and my sister
rinsing the stink from her hair
with a warm wash
rattles her nails
and squeezing her tresses
comes up and into the comfort
of a terrycloth turban

what is it the mirror
will tell her tomorrow

for it's been
fifty years since then
though it's only two days
and counting
from the hour
when Lebanon
broke open the heart of a distant morning
as it was once with Halifax
and Hiroshima, Coventry
and Dresden and the firestorms
of Gomorrah

my uncle looking up
from his dinner
and smiling
the first day he realized
though he'd been blinded for weeks
what a blessing it was
to see again
what the spirit sees when the body lets go

The Thousand Tears

when my beloved grandmother passed
her four daughters
sorted through
what was left
of her life's possessions
and each
in her own way
grieved the loss
with a generosity of keepsakes
I think it must be Mary
who has
the bone-china horses
the high-spirited hind-leg
palomino stallions
fired to glory with a blond glaze
of mane set out on a whatnot shelf
at the farm
and who's for the doilies
stained like wet snowflakes
Queen Anne's lace
with a prick-fingered purple
ink dash at the exact centre of the tatting
who's for the caftan
the warm-in-the-winter
throes, orange as autumn gourds
the antimacassars
the tattered rugs
the Tommy Hunter records
the old TV

but when the Busteed girls
conspired to pour
the only uncapped forty ounce
bottle of Canadian Club
down the sink
because "surely it will be spoiled"
teetotaler's conviction
my father

leapt into action
as you would were it a live
German hand grenade
or a handle-with-care
wash of nitroglycerine
something volatile

"it must be skunky by now"
was the theory

though I'm left wondering
where went that thirsty dram

who drank
that single shot

that's the mystery
a thousand tears away from being solved

Ode on Homemade Wine at Christmas

not since that drunken Christmas
of my childhood
when we came home
from my maternal grandfather's
most abstemious and loving house
to find
the hired man Thomas Sheil Malott
in a bony shambles
lying wrecked upon the dining room floor
with my mother's
Irish lace tablecloth pulled from the Maplewood sideboard
and draping his frame
like a first communion
poor Tom, he'd been left alone too long
in late December weather
having found my uncle's private cellar
fermented on the farm
oh, the dandelion harvest of the lawn
oh the time-softened tomato crop of the garden
and the small wild blue Concord
foxing the grape of the vine
with a musky fragrance of fruit rot
anything at all put to the purpose of the cordial
in the drunkard's pump-house jugs

not since then
have I given much consideration
to wine at Christmas
webbed in old cellars of memory
darkening down to the fever in the drink
when the mind in the moment becomes
both the thinker and the thought you think

The Physics of Memory, the Mechanics of Dream

does the memory
of last year's apple crop
not always dawdle in the orchard
within the wine scent
of an ever-enduring earth
receiving her windfalls as they drop
or does it not linger
in the apple basket in the basement
below the stairs
where time's visible thief
goes stealing through present shadow
into the bruise hollows
of a scab-skinned russet or softening spy
first sending its halo of fruit flies
in their looming hungers hovering
over brown orbs
rotting under winter weight
of the long darkness of an early dusk
what with the autumn harvest
long past perduring
there in the cider redolence ripening sweet
for the butterfly sinks his long proboscis
in the cut wedge of nectar come alive in
a grateful flex of orange-and-black wings

though memory, however real
however true, will not stir
even an empty cup a quarter inch from stasis
whereas dream
might spill the glass entire
with the flung free hand of the sleeper
who remembers everything
in the half-life of a small loss
though he wake to thirst and weeping

What Holds Us When We're Gone

my father milked our cow with care and ease
his strong hands stroking the teats
with the expertise of a master
so the stream of milk
striking the inner hollow
of the silver pail would sound
the bell at first with a drumming gong
like the coming of rain
to a metal roof and then
with a foaming slosh
of liquid warmth
that soaked the rising surface
like bubbled soap
and there in the barn
at the gutter end of the stanchion with
the jersey stamping flies
the cats would gather in a hungry choir
and my father would aim a single strand
so it shot through the air
striking the open-mouth face
with a sweet gargle of pleasure
and the lucky tom would swallow hard
then groom his whiskers
for the white tears that clung like webs of dew
and I know
he did it for me
he performed to amuse
his son who loved the cats

and I remember as well the ritual
before the milking began
the fogging of flies
the cleaning away of the stray straws
that clung to the belly girthed by ribs
the greasing of teats
the placing of the one-legged stool
the leaning in
so his hat crushed against the flank
like that of shy suitor
and then the concentration of hands
the quick and steady strength of hands
as the slushy music of liquefied rhythms
moved through changes and variations
like listening to water on rock
and there in the cream line
of a fine result
with a thought for the house
and a thought for the churn
a thought for the thermos
we carried to school
a thought for the taste
of the graze in summer-green grass and
a thought
for the corn-silage flavour of winter

and like the fourth fold
on a care-filled page
I've written the most secret names
with a thought
for the sweet-souled earth
how it holds us in
when we're gone

Vinegar on the lips of the Lord

my father walked
like an old-world-worker
crossing the yard on the farm
his body yoked by two white
wire-handled ten-gallon pails
proud of his strength
even at eighty
he was strong-shouldered
his rain-stained
loose-laced leather boots
the colour of oak leaf
in late November
he smiles and sets his burden
where it sinks in the earth
crushing the grass
in a green circle of bent blades
as proof of tomorrow
in what we manage today
and then
as time also worries the wool
of a ewe after last lambing
her fleece
come away at the fences
like sorrowful smoke
he entered the final weakening
the one that comes to us all
with that hospital shuffle
in a blue johnny gown
with its gap at the back
his appetite
dwindled to applesauce
in a single spoon
the sour-sweet silver flavour of it
sufficient as it is with
the vinegar my uncle calls *mother*

he shows me the word
in his own big dictionary
in the den
draws my attention
to the caring in the language
and there it is that word
like a sip of water when the lips are dry

What Can You See When It's Gone

when you look to the top of the hill
where the barns
used to be on the farm
those black buildings
loom in the mind
dark memory
that billows
where phantom storm stains an old sky
like the oil you can't wash
from blue cloth

and the ghost fog of sheep
are grazing gone grass
and eating the windfalls away
where the tree lost its apples
in autumn
one thought at a time

if the mist in the meadow
is cold in the winter
as frost that clings to wet wool
and warm
in the vanishing dawn
was it there
like a voice from the grave
both the wind in the weather
that worries the rain
in the name on a stone
and the name it is wearing away …

near Melbourne Australia
in the forests of night
they found a wild ram
gone blind in his burden of wool
his fleece curling over his face full as thunder

and oh when you're lost
and oh, when you're found
can you see
where you were
when where you once were isn't there

Renovation

the carpenter
blinded the window and
blocked up the door
so the cranberry glass
at the top of the wall
lost all the light
that had once come
splintering into the room
in shattered beams
staining the floor
like spilled wine and broken glass
now concealed in darkness
like Forutnato's mind
and then
a bricked-in portal
always obvious from the porch side
of the house
appearing there shaped
in off-colour clay
like a mason's error
an architectural flaw
where ancestors
with ghostly hands
might claw
the frame like fog
through branches or smoke
come out of deep fire
grown hot in combustible cloth

that farmhouse
transformed by time
to the fallen kitchen
and the vestal concerns
of the orchard and the garden
of the scalding shed
and the killing tree
and the meat locker in the village
that farmhouse
with its insatiable appetite for ghosts
like mist on a mirror
or frost on cold glaze

this then
is the sad silence
of a closed piano
the Queen Anne legs
put to a second purpose
under the harvest table
a sorrowful quiet
for the lost daughter
waked in the room
shut up for winter
draped in white linen
and waiting for spring

The Conversation

we sat on the hill
overlooking the lake
discussing the rebuilding
of broken-down barns
how he'd jacked a sagging wall
and called the rain
away from where it soaked the wood
so it went punk
as an old book
gone pulpy in the pages
sunk to the end-boards
in storm swell and wet weather
his lamentation
including the north-east corner
that foundered
like a great ship
causing a near subsidence
of a fieldstone foundation
the dry rock come tumbling like scree
or heaved up and out
like a frost-shrugged boulder
so it lay cantilevered
above a fractured lintel
and oh
how the wilderness
wants it gone
this man-made structure
punched through by sumac and
weed phylum of green things
with water-greedy roots
muscling over the floor
and raw leaves nettling for nutrients
in lime-stained earth

and just then
a single cicada
sang out in the willow overhead
a high-pitched whine
a metallic flang of shredded noise
like wind-torn tin
ripped crooked and shrieking
from a sharp-edge saw

and we listened
as though
to a list of reasons
Luna moth, katydid
Carolina locust, darning-needle fly,
lacewing, monarch, preying mantis, grasshopper
crickets so small
they slip through the screening
of a boy's insect project
Cecropia, Polyphemus
the blind-winged moths
battering candle shadow
and constellations of glowworms
winking in brilliant galaxies of grass
and smouldering swarms of midges
haunting the treetops
in spiritual drifts like eidolons of nightfall

and no one
but the strong-shouldered
ghosts of summer
to hold them there
hovering in lost rafters of absent heaven
and coming down
in dusty shafts of shimmering light

Bereft

there's a cosmic zero in this stone
like frosted ice
grey shale's enough
to make a school of rock
as self-instructive slate
gives life to time
red oxygen's a water rot
within the iron's underside
like blood within the earth

this slim shelf struck free
from the lonesome season when
the sea withdrew its sheltering salt
and creatures
gasped in shallow welts of air
their gills orgasmic
as the waves retreat
in foamy strands
the frothy afterthought
of moon pools
lit by morning shine
as linen thins away or
cotton rubbed to rags becomes
a slow reveal of weave
the threaded crosshatch of the loom

cold heaven in a meteoric rage
strikes this escarpment
like a clock of shattering stars
to stun the mind
that sees the midnight sky
in fractured brilliance at a single glance

last night I dreamed
my father
and his brother
both alive within a dark amaze
to see them vanish as I woke

Afterword

It has been a royal delight working with John over the years. I have called him Johnny, Mr. B., hey you, and brother. John and I worked together on this Hidden Brook Press series of books called the John B. Lee Signature Series, beginning with the first three publications in 2017. In the interim, we published twelve very fine books. I told each and every one of the authors in the JBL Signature Series, "If you work with John as your editor, I will, hands down, publish your book." This commitment of mine is testament to how much I admire and how deeply trust John as an acquisitions editor of the aforementioned series. Never has he let me down, neither as an editor, nor as a friend.

I said to John as I was about to retire from my thirty year stint as publisher of HBP that I found myself in a bit of a pickle, what with having sold HBP before I could publish the thirteenth book in the series. I had insisted that the final book be John's own book, thereby making That Isn't You the capstone of a very fine CanLit series. So, here we are with this final book in the series, and it is the first book to be published by the new owner of HBP who is coincidentally also named John, but his is a head with a different hat.

But back to the pickle: This particular John, that is to say John B. Lee, said to me of my situation, by way of quoting Arlo Guthrie "I don't want a pickle, I just wanna ride my motorcycle." "Don't sweat it, John B.. I'll happily work with the new owners of HBP if they will work with me." The proverbial pickle has been removed from the jar. And with the publication of That Isn't You, we have a perfect capstone for the John B. Lee Signature Series and with that a new start for HBP. My prediction is that the JBLSS with this as a capstone will leave an indelible mark on the CanLit landscape. I am proud to have been the publisher of the Signature Series. It has been an honour to work with this three-time Poet Laureate, the author of over seventy titles - John B. Lee.

Richard (Tai) Grove

Author Bio

In 2005 John B. Lee was inducted as Poet Laureate of Brantford in perpetuity. The same year he received the distinction of being named Honourary Life Member of The Canadian Poetry Association and The Ontario Poetry Society. In 2007 he was made a member of the Chancellor's Circle of the President's Club of McMaster University and named first recipient of the Souwesto Award for his contribution to literature in his home region of southwestern Ontario and he was named winner of the inaugural Black Moss Press Souwesto Award for his contribution to the ethos of writing in Southwestern Ontario. In 2005 he was appointed Poet Laureate of the city of Brantford in perpetuity. In 2011 he was appointed Poet Laureate of Norfolk County (2011-14) and in 2015 Honourary Poet Laureate of Norfolk County for life and in 2017 he received a Canada 150 Medal from the Federal Government of Canada for "his outstanding contribution to literary development both at home and abroad." A recipient of over eighty prestigious international awards for his writing he is winner of the $10,000 CBC Literary Award for Poetry, the only two time recipient of the People's Poetry Award, and 2006 winner of the inaugural Souwesto Orison Writing Award (University of Windsor). In 2007 he was named winner of the Winston Collins Award for Best Canadian Poem, an award he won again in 2012. He has well-over seventy books published to date and is the editor of twenty anthologies including two best-selling works: That Sign of Perfection: poems and stories on the game of hockey; and Smaller Than God: words of spiritual longing. He co-edited a special issue of Windsor Review—Alice Munro: A Souwesto Celebration published in the fall of 2014. As a translator he is credited with co-translating the seminal anthology Sweet Cuba: The Building of a Poetic Tradition: 1608-1958 (Hidden Brook Press, 2010). In 2020 he was appointed Poet Laureate of the Canada Cuba Literary Alliance. His work has appeared internationally in over 500 publications, and has been translated into French, Spanish, Korean, Bosnian, Hindi and Chinese. He has read his work in nations all over the world including South Africa, France, Korea, Cuba, Canada and the United States. He has received letters of praise from Nelson Mandela, Desmond Tutu, Australian Poet, Les Murray, and Senator Romeo Dallaire. Called "the greatest living poet in English," by poet George Whipple, he lives in a lake house overlooking Long Point Bay in Port Dover, Ontario where he works as a full time author.

www.ingramcontent.com/pod-product-compliance
Lightning Source LLC
Chambersburg PA
CBHW050259120526
44590CB00016B/2414